Best wishes to my dutiful
surgeon and friend, Larry
Frank.
1/2001

PUBLISHED BY

The Barrios Trust
Victorian Legal Center
653 Eleventh Street
Oakland, California 94607-3650

Poetry can be perceived
as threads of inspired thought
like the warp and the weft,
woven into a meaningful fabric.

DEDICATION

I dedicate the poetry in this anthology
to my mother, Mary Louise Wilson,
and adopt as my pen name,
her maiden name, Barrios.

~ Warren Barrios Wilson

INTRODUCTION

This anthology embraces the weathervane
of my mind, of a variety of thoughts and feelings
in the human spirit and experience.

It is with enthusiasm and pleasure that I share
them with others entertaining an open spirit.

~ Barrios

Romance

Reflections

HUMOR

SPIRITUAL

ROMANCE

JOANNE

Bright of spirit
eyes so clear
Friendly speaking
with others near

How to describe
her warmth and grace
Ingenuous expression
in every face!

Moppet head
with curly hair
Irish to be sure
fixed in place

Home and hostess
in remarkable blend
Gourmet food
for every friend

With Helen's lead
and mother's lace
She Casey guides
in every chase

With depth that's like
the Irish Sea
and open heart
she came to me

My love for her
my heart she sends
Romantically we meld
and blend

My aging spirit
kept in mind
her gentle self
is always kind

And reaching forth
in destiny
our fabric threads
in unity

ALLEGRO

Contrapuntal
     poet gay
Words so rhythmic
     play and say

Music dancing
     notes a-prancing
Rise and fall
     along the way

Ride the waves
     heed not the sage
Leaves go falling
     page by page

Freely bodies
     following sound
Distant music
     round and round

Touch my gentle
           heart in flight
Moving shadows
           fluttering light

Hold me closely
           lest my fear
Overwhelms me
           deathlike near

Renew the spirits'
           endless dance
As I pray
           the night away

INTIMACY

We are no longer the words
    We are the symphony
Without score, without conductor
    And the music plays
With the melody synchronizing
    In harmony, in beauty, completely

We need each other now
    To sense our fingertips touching
Lightly, gently, freely
    Layers and layers of feeling

Prelude, inspiration, patiently
    Awaiting brilliant flowers
Blooming gloriously, unfolding
    In a romantic concerto

Only I, only You, only We
    Can hear and understand
The theme, suffused
    Playing for all time.

THE BARD

Mood, feeling, rising slowly,
  Thoughts flowing softly, lightly,

Vibrantly rising, irresistibly,
  Uncontrollably, unrelentingly,

Aware, subjectively, self aware
  As the score appears, visibly

Coherently formed, and understood
  By the other, appreciatively,

Fulfillingly, even as he
  Is fulfilled, expressed, completely.

CASEY

'Twas with moppet
    curly hair
That an Irish lass
    so fair

'Cross the table
    from me sat
On that morning
    that we met

And her eyes
    so bold and clear
Caught my fancy
    and my stare

While the theme
    of Gloccamora
And the cliffs
    at Galway Bay

Crossed my mind
    And touched my spirit
As we talked
    so long that day

How was I
        to know that she
In my heart
        would come to be
Like the light
        at Irish Sea

And in my golden
        days would bear
Another Casey lass
        with flare

Who with bright gleam
        in her eye
Would come dashing
        and a-flashing
Like a meteor
        'cross my sky

Now when the Casey
        clan does gather
And their blarney
        fills the air

Sure 'tis a bit
        of Ireland
And its joy
        that we all share

PRELUDE

Warm, friendly feelings
  Buds opening, slowly, gently
Eyes, meeting other eyes, deeply
  Fingers touching, finger tips, lightly
Words, soft words, warm words
  Voices, speaking, eagerly
Hearts, beating, faster
  Flowers opening, wider, beautifully
Thoughts revealing, hidden feelings
  Prelude, anxious, moments bursting
Through long winter shadows, fading
  Fingers, squeezing, clutching
Desperately, other fingers, hands
  Lips, quivering lips, softly
Sipping, lingering liquid tongues
  Music, sweeping, strains, playing
Romantic, blending, dancing, moving
  Warm bodies, touching, caressing
Blazing, brilliant flowers, blooming!!!

MISTY

Nymph, rising from the mist
Provoked by the music of the Bard
Dancing freely, for the first time
Released to be, and see herself
As only he, likewise, is free
To be his love, and waltz with him
In a romantic symphony.

OPENERS

A woman with poise
And standing tall
Beneath their feet
Her wax did fall

Hands made to touch
And mold the clay
In shapes and forms
that flow and sway

In reaching forth
To reach the mold
Their fingers touched
With palms unfold

Their eyes then met
And spirits danced
Unwittingly in
Light romance

Her sculptured work
He learned to know
One studio noon
That moved him so

The Bard then read
And matched her mood
While fingers swiftly
Sketched his head

The paint then flowed
In colors deep
While capturing a strength
that she did seek

'Tho space and time
Has passed them by
Those haunting hands
Still fill his eye

CASEY LOUISE

Not sweet fourteen
but a shadowy beauty
poised and serene

Needs space to grow
in solitude
different from familiar
flowers that we know

Who will she be
this willowy sapling
that we see?

Her unfurled petals
will bloom and grow
in sunlight and shadow
we soon will know

An athlete strong
she strives to be
in sports she thrives
that all may see

To books she turns
reluctantly
then says with pride
and now I'm free

R E N E W A L

Like the hummingbird
       with wings that swirl
From distance far
       and light my world

With feathers flashing
       allegro dancing
And sips the nectar
       its beak romancing

A Bard did come
       from distance far
And light the shadows
       of my brooding star

Poetically in romance
       and rhyme
Our fingers touched
       a moment in time

Now in quiet nights
       in woods around
My spirit is filled
       with light and sound

VERONICA

Hands so nimble
    fast and quick
Fingers supple
    busily pick

Mushrooms sprouting
    round and round
Emerging suddenly
    without a sound

'Neath the branches
    In the woods
So rarely seen and understood

Berries sprouting
    here and there
Bushes bursting everywhere

Bears a-picking
    by her side
Fearlessly she
    does not hide

Playmates as they
    swing and sway
Morning sunshine
    lights the way

Legend lady
    known afar
Always reaching
    for a star

Beautiful symbol
    for us all
Nature's lady
    spring or fall

I but see her
    passing by
In fleeting moments
    she lights my sky

Grateful for her
    presence near
Ever buoyant
    eyes so clear

Will she always
    find her way
In the woods
    that light her day?

SANTORINI SAPPHIRE

Mystic glistening beauty
    of volcanic eruption

Sapphire gleaming gem
    of the Helenic Isles

Provacative Princess of
    the anima and animus

Erotic sensual sounder
    of Hero and Heroine's sea

Meditteranean Queen
    of the Greek Isle paradise

Poet's frustrated lover of
    uncaptured verse and rhyme

White Knight's sword point
    of the Golden Fleece

Imprisoned captive of
    Minotaur's restless mind

Could Mozart, Beethoven
    or Bach have orchestrated you?

Or does your symphonic music
    flow without conductor or score?

Could Shakespeare have
        framed you with his sonnets?

Could Neruda have
        embodied you in his love poems?

Do you need the sun, the moon
        or the stars to enhance you?

Could Zorba have distanced you
        from his phallus
        while serenading you on his santuri?

Could even Zeus' erotic dreams
        have given birth to you?

As you proudly stand
        postured in the marine light,
        immortally bred by nature's grandeur

Are you the eternal Muse
        awaiting the romantic depth
        of an inspired poet
        to phrase and capture you

And write of the exciting pulse
        and passion of your heartbeat?

Only then will you become
        the universal Goddess of mankind.

MOMENTARY MOOD

In moments when
My thoughts do flow
To evening's past
Warm afterglow

A room apart
Awake I lie
With need to touch
And hear her sigh

My spirit yields
In fantasy
To part of her
That responds to me

'Cross miles of space
That between us lies
My heart beats slow
In sober vow

Then turns in quiet
Sleep for now

AFTERGLOW

When artificial
       barriers loom
Like mountains in
       the afterglow

My melancholy
       spirit speaks
And in my heart
       a message flows

"No distance, time
       nor space can bar
The light and beauty
       of its star"

Transcending cliffs
       that gather round
Are ladders to
       a higher ground

IN MEMORABILIA

If time stood still
>When moments focused

On feelings shared
>When spirits touched

The morning dew
>of fresh anticipation

In hearts that quickened
>in friendships new

My soul inspired
>Would speak and say,

"Oh devil time,
>take not away

The dawning of
>this brilliant day."

HAIL TO THE ARTIST

To you sensitive, creative people
Who translate feeling into imagery
And ennoble our lives and our spirits
By lifting them above the mundane
To a more meaningful measure
Of our world, our community, ourselves

To you often neglected souls
Who labor tirelessly in the vineyard
Despite our not infrequent neglect
To express our interest and concern
In you and your inspiring work

Thank you for sharing
Your best with all of us;
Thank you for following
Your inspiration and your vision,
Recognition not withstanding

To you, we give honor
And extend our praise.
To you, we extend our appreciation.
To you, we pay tribute!

PHALLUS LAMENT

Oh, pounding waves
That beat the shore
Am I to ever
Know thee more?

In moments of uncertainty
Will ever I be
A raging sea?

In thy design
Am I to find
Thy incessant power
No longer mine.

Can Animus transcend
with Psyche's aid
My hero's spirit
Now afraid?

On distant shore
Will I still roam
And not within
Thy breaker's foam?

Oh, inner eye
That lights the sky
My restless soul
Still questions why

Will peacefully
My spirit be
When Phallus rod
Is bent in me?

Yea, sheath thy sword
And Warrior's pride,
Find peace within
The Ebbing tide

That speaks to thee
With sweet content
And quiet thy
Poor heart's lament

SEPTEMBER MOOD

When light grows dim
And vision blurs
When ringing ear
Within doth sound

When Minotaur's maze
And boundary line
A narrow path
Encircles mine

I reach beyond
My earth confined
And seek a highway
To the sea

There where the ocean
waves unfurl
And light the shadows
In my world

FIRE

Combustion, ignition, spark, flame,
    blaze, wind and fire, fear

Sweeping force of energy,
    Wildfire, conflagration, holocaust

Man, reckless builder and destroyer
    of Nature's Garden of Eden

Victim of misplaced energy
    When God, supreme above all

Enlightened Man, in humility,
    grace and spirit of fellowship

Nurturer, sustainer of plant and flower,
    of fireside, hearth and family

And the warmth and beauty
    of the earth that spawns him

And the bloom and flower
    of our lives

Dominion, love, harmony
    and peace is his

IT'S TIME NOW

It's time now, Man
     When you've got to go with it
Right now, Man, when
     There's no more show in it
It's time now, Man

It's time now, Man
     When the stuff's not doin' it
Even now, Man, when
     Your arm keeps fuckin' it
It's time now, Man

When the deal's so bad
     That the bile's got shit in it
And the smile looks sad
     Even with guile in it
It's time now, Man

It's time now, Man
     When the pain's still tough in ya
Even tho' she's there
     And keeps on suckin' ya
It's time now, Man

It's time now, Man
        When the deck's so stacked
That the Dealer just smiles
        No matter what's in your act
It's time now, Man

It's time now, Man
        When that mountain's just ahead
And you're givin' it all
        While the body's just goin' dead
It's time now, Man

It's time now, Man
        When there's no more place to run
And the flesh's turning cold
        Even lying there in the sun
It's time now, Man

L I O N E L

The first to spring forth
    from Jules and Louise
A child of great promise
    and likely to please

With a glow of New Orleans
    upon his face
He was reaching out early
    for a star in his space

A toddler's slow gait
    he could not see
An athlete's pace
    was his to be

With a ball in his hand
    not with his right but his left
He began to play catch
    and toss it with zest

With a battered old raquet
    and Zelda his friend
On the tennis court he rallied
    from end to end

Carving a pathway in sports
    for his siblings to follow
A champion at best
    with modesty blessed

The mountains of race
    that did early surround
Were ladders he climbed
    to find higher ground

A soldier of fortune
    he wanted to be
The roar of the crowd
    was his destiny

Strong in mind and body
    he found sports as his place
A winner he was
    in every race

A scholar without a book
    in his hand
Good skills he developed
    in becoming a man

Sadly from sports
    he then turned away
Though with DiMaggio grace
    he could field and play

The racial barriers
    refused to yield
And no blacks in baseball
    could then break the seal

To the law he turned
    with his brilliant mind
And a remarkable career
    he was there to find

From lawyer to judge
    he soon made his way
For others to follow
    in a brighter day

As his cities' black leader
    he wanted to see
From political bondage
    his people set free

With friends and supporters
　　at his side
Into the Mayor's race
　　he did confidently stride

As Mayor and leader
　　city council in hand
His city did grow
　　and opportunity expand

And now with it over
　　his mantle now passed
His name and his fame
　　with others still lasts

Like the star that he grasped
　　as a child long ago
Flowers now bloom
　　in the light of his glow

And now, Hi Mayor! Hi Judge!
　　Hi Lionel they say,
Within the city he loves
　　As he walks on his way

ODE TO THE TBM MAPMAKERS

You are the warp threads
and the weft threads
In the fabric of the Company

Increasingly weaving
in line, color, arc
and map imagery

A dramatic, visible garment
with easy path to follow
Street upon street,
highway upon highway
freeway upon freeway

Street guides, wall maps,
and road atlases flow
in creative design

Bringing us fame and fortune
      as you continue rowing in concert
while building a leading team

Confidently striding forward
      venturing west to east
and south to north
with cartography in mind

In gratitude we pay tribute
      to you seamless map makers
Honoring the streetscape
      of your scene

BARCELONA SIN DON QUIXOTE

As I walk the Carreras here
        without Don Quixote to liven my mind
Neither Picasso, Miro nor Gaudi
        as a Hero do I find

Even thoughts of abuelo Zaragoza
        seem distant and far away
As I struggle with "pigeon" Spanish
        in striving to know what to say

But with Michelin to Guide me
        it's not IBM's for sure
And with Langenscheidt in my pocket
        I feel enthusiastic and secure

Until my ear hears Cataluña
        and I see it written on the signs
And my steps begin to falter
        as I strive to make it mine

But as I stroll along the Ramblas
         with families at my side
I get excited as I watch the
         Mimes and Pajaros on the rise

Then the antiquity of Laietana
         takes me ages back in time
And my spirit soars in beauty
         of its original design

And I hear within a symphony
         as art and romance fill my mind
And idioma not withstanding
         an inner vision clears in rhyme

So even without ole Don Quixote
         and the great who've gone before
Just being here in Barcelona
         has my heart captured by its lore

REDEEMING GRACE MORE THAN A FACE

Delightful dishes
    artfully spread
In front of him
    at the table head

Kimono-clad lady
    graceful and shy
Obviously misleading
    the guy
With chopsticks stirring
    the tureen a-purring

Shining black hair
    with sprigs of flowers
Candlelight framing
    a face so rare

Had I seen her
    passing by
Could I but love her
    'til I die?

And knowing her
    would want to see
My Japanese lady
    with spirit free

B O U N T I F U L

Curving marshmallow mounds
    Circles, rounded lines
Earthly rolling hills
    Ever visible signs

Playmates for another
    Apollo or his brother

Aphrodite would lead
    Hungry mouths to feed
Stallions shaking heads
    Tearing at the threads

Mobiles as they sway
    Ever in the way

Sculptured shapes and forms
    Inviting as they stand
Waiting for her man
    To mold them in his hand

THE BRIDGE BETWEEN

The pathway to
the Golden star
So distant now
from where we are
Lies just beyond
the Bridge Between

Loved ones despairingly
standing by
While transcending sense
reveals a sign

Of deliverance from
fear and pain that bind
In my search for
the Bridge Between

Inspired thought
Soul doth reveal
Piercing the shadow
that sense conceals
On the spiritual pathway to
the Bridge Between

Along the way, Mind's
light doth guide
Unerring footsteps to
the other side beyond
the Bridge Between

A distant star now
lights the night
And mist no longer
clouds my sight to
the Bridge Between

The arms of Love
embrace me now
With promises fulfilled
and there is no
Bridge Between

CROSSROAD

Oh miracle of Life,
Whose grand design I see
In unity with Mind
Originated me

The Human and divine
Coincidence of mine
Is the beginning of the truth
Of life in which I shine

My path unfolds anew
And opens wide the way
The portals of my spirit
In every dawning day

The clangor in the sound
I hear from every side
Becomes a symphony of Soul
Enriching me around

The crucible of life
And death along my path
Disperses as a storm
In love that knows no wrath

Approaching the cross-road
The bridge ahead seems dim,
When suddenly I know
That I am one with Him.

INVOCATION

I include all of you,
and you include me

Together, we are one
Separately, we stand in darkness

In prayer and reverence,
we champion each other

As I embrace you,
I enrapture myself

Bonded, we rejoice
and acclaim our union

Yield to my entreaty
Come with me

United we stand strong
and face our destiny

Eternity, we await you
confidently

Peter Boiger

MADRE DE LA TIERRA

Earth mother,
        womb of the universe
Mystic lady of la Tierra
        past, present, and future
Generations yet unborn

Stately fountain, Genesis
        from which flows all life,
Compassionate mother
        of us all

As we glorify Thee
        we pay tribute to ourselves
And our indivisible
        connection to each other

Angel, spiritual inspiration
        of goodness and blessing
Of offspring of her womb

Creator, animating Principle
        of us all,
Essential womanhood
        embracing us,
To Thee we give glory,
        to Thee we pay tribute.

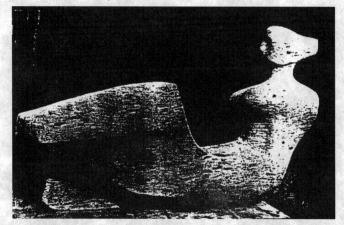

Peter Boiger

MADRE DE LA TIERRA

Tierra Madre,
     vientre del universo
Dama mística de la Tierra
     pasado, presente y futuro
Generaciones toda vía no nacidas

Magestuosa fuente, Genesis
     de donde corre toda la vida,
Compasiva madre
     de tos nosotros

Mientras nosotros glorificamos a usted
     nos rendimos homenaje a nosotros mismos
Y nuestra indivisible
     conexion a cada uno

Angel, espiritual inspiracion
     de bondad y bendiciones
De hijos de su vientre

Creador, Principio animador
     de todos nosotros,
Estado esencial de mujer
     abrasandonos,
A Usted le damos gloria,
     a Usted le rendimos homenaje.

TIME AND SEASON

Seize the moment
Seize the time
Let your spirit
Flow in rhyme

Let the burning
Chalice flame
Light thy path
And speak thy name

Childlike listening
On the plain
Reap and sow
The harvest grain

Voices ringing laud
And clear
With His presence
Ever near
Prayerfully we
Seek and find
Timelessly the fertile vine

ON BROTHERHOOD

Brotherhood, and its spirit
of fellowship

Threads and weaves a fabric
with brilliant, eternal fiber

Into a web of feeling
and emotion and gratitude

That sustains, fulfills and inspires
like the light of

A brilliant, distant dawn
breaking through the

Shadows of the remnant
clouds of a dark night.

It presses like sunbeams
in the morning dew

Of tears, and pain and sorrow
midst awakening of hope

Of a better, brighter today
and more fulfilling tomorrow

And hands grasping other hands'
warm and friendly fingers

Indivisibly bonded within
an inseparable union

Rejoice in a brotherly affection
And the mortal dream brightens.

Yosemite

Grand Cathedrals
in divine doxology

Rising Sentinels
from foaming river rock

Spiritual symphony
in chords of harmony

Cascading sound rising
from solid sculptured stone

Majestic testimonial
of which Man
can scarcely speak

Wither the voice within
to prayerfully acclaim
thy creative splendor?

Gratitude closeted
in the mist
Beholding the glory of
thy infinite design

MOTHER AFRICA

Your restless, haunting soul,
  precursor of the life
  of all mankind

Still permeates the troubled
  consciousness, feelings, and
  emotions of the progeny
  of your enslavers

The magnitude and immensity
  of the continental expanse
  within the grandeur
  of your resplendent ecosystem

Of desert, sand, mountains
  and tropical jungle
  permeated with its
  rare, incomparable wildlife
  captures and fascinates

All who witness and behold
  your breathtaking symmetry
  and the soulful beat
  and rhythm of your
  dynamic, ebony people

A LIGHT ANEW

He came with the
   wings of angels
   In the dawn
   of a starlit morn

We herald him
   as a messenger
   Of the Christ
   that lights our way

He communed with
   spiritual leaders
   As a child
   with vision clear

And demonstrated
   the healing Christ
   with the sick,
   the lame and the blind

He recognized
   the source within
   as the power
   and presence of Mind

He revealed
   a Lord's prayer
   to inspire us
   'round him gathered
   on the Mount divine

And proved life
   to be infinite
   and deathless
   in the Father's grand design

With his teachings
   of truth to guide us
   from ignorance and bondage
   he set us free

Enabling us
   to demonstrate
   a new reality

With enlightened
   divine awareness
   he overcame cross
   and death and tomb

Appearing in the
morning light thereafter
on the shores
of the Galilean sea

To his followers
in resurrection
his scarred body
for them to see

And now our
hearts can sing
because death
has lost its sting

And fear no more
can rule us
because of our mighty King.